Short Stories for Students, Volume 22

Project Editor: Ira Mark Milne

Editorial: Sara Constantakis, Anne Marie Hacht, Gillian Leonard **Rights Acquisition and Management**: Emma Hull, Sue Rudolph, Andrew Specht **Manufacturing**: Drew Kalasky

Image Research & Acquisition: Kelly A. Quin **Imaging and Multimedia**: Lezlie Light, Dan Newell **Product Design**: Pamela A. E. Galbreath **Vendor Administration**: Civie Green

Product Manager: Meggin Condino

For more information, contact
Gale, an imprint of Cengage Learning
27500 Drake Rd.
Farmington Hills, MI 48331-3535

Or you can visit our Internet site at
http://www.gale.com

ALL RIGHTS RESERVED
No part of this work covered by the copyright
hereon may be reproduced or used in any form or
by any means—graphic, electronic, or mechanical,
including photocopying, recording, taping, Web
distribution, or information storage retrieval
systems—without the written permission of the
publisher.

For permission to use material from this product,
submit your request via Web at http://www.gale-
edit.com/permissions, or you may download our
Permissions Request form and submit your request
by fax or mail to: *Permissions Department*
Gale, an imprint of Cengage Learning
27500 Drake Rd.
Farmington Hills, MI 48331-3535

Permissions Hotline:
248-699-8006 or 800-877-4253, ext. 8006
Fax: 248-699-8074 or 800-762-4058

Since this page cannot legibly accommodate all
copyright notices, the acknowledgments constitute
an extension of the copyright notice.

While every effort has been made to ensure the
reliability of the information presented in this
publication, Gale, an imprint of Cengage Learning
does not guarantee the accuracy of the data
contained herein. Gale, an imprint of Cengage
Learning accepts no payment for listing; and
inclusion in the publication of any organization,

agency, institution, publication, service, or individual does not imply endorsement of the editors or publisher. Errors brought to the attention of the publisher and verified to the satisfaction of the publisher will be corrected in future editions.

ISBN 0-7876-7030-8
ISSN 1092-7735

Printed in the United States of America
10 9 8 7 6 5 4 3 2 1

The Pearl

John Steinbeck 1947

Introduction

In *The Log from "The Sea of Cortez"* Steinbeck writes that he heard a story about a Mexican boy finding a huge pearl and thinking that he would never have to work again. Soon, however, so many people tried to take the pearl from him that he threw it back into the sea. The story so struck his imagination that he created his own version of it in his celebrated novella *The Pearl*. Steinbeck changed the boy into the adult Kino, and gave him a family, and created a compelling story of oppression, rebellion, and greed.

After Kino finds the largest and most beautiful pearl he has ever seen, he is convinced that it will ensure him and his family a promising future. He will be able to have enough money to cure his son Coyotito from the poison of a scorpion's bite, to marry Coyotito's mother, and to provide his son with an education, which he knows will help him to escape the bonds of the oppression under which his people suffer. Kino does not count, however, on the power of the pearl to inspire the worst as well as the best in human nature.

Author Biography

John Steinbeck Jr. was born in Salinas, California, on February 27, 1902. His father John served as the county treasurer in Salinas. His mother Olive was a school teacher and helped inspire her son's passion for reading. In the summers during his youth, Steinbeck worked on nearby ranches as a hired hand. This work cultivated his love for the earth, which emerges in so many of his works.

After high school, Steinbeck attended Stanford University between 1920 and 1926, where he studied marine biology but did not earn a degree. After moving to New York, he determined to make a career out of writing. He worked briefly as a reporter for the *American* before deciding to return to California.

For the next couple of years, he took on odd jobs to support himself while he wrote. He worked as a painter, fruit picker, and surveyor, among other professions. Steinbeck wrote his first novel in 1929, *Cup of Gold*, which was not well received. His next two novels, *The Pastures of Heaven*, published in 1932, and *To a God Unknown*, published the next year, were also unsuccessful.

In 1930, Steinbeck and his first wife, Carol Henning, moved to Pacific Grove where he gathered material for his first successful novel, *Tortilla Flat*, a humorous story about Mexican Americans. It earned Steinbeck the California

Commonwealth Club's Gold Medal for best novel by a California author. The 1937 novel *Of Mice and Men* established his literary reputation as one of America's finest novelists. Steinbeck's most celebrated work, *The Grapes of Wrath*, published in 1939, earned him the Pulitzer Prize. The book was later made into a film by John Ford and became one of the American Film Institute's top 100 classic films.

During World War II, Steinbeck wrote war propaganda and worked briefly as a war correspondent for the *New York Herald Tribune*. Some of his dispatches were later collected and published with the title, *Once There Was a War*. He wrote the screenplay for Alfred Hitchcock's film *Lifeboat* in 1944. After the war, he wrote two more successful works, *Cannery Row* (1945), and *The Pearl* (1947).

In his later years, he tried to reclaim his waning status as a major American novelist with works such as *Burning Bright* (1950), *East of Eden* (1952), and *The Winter of Our Discontent* (1961). None of these novels, however, gained Steinbeck the praise his earlier works received. Yet, in 1962, Steinbeck was awarded the Nobel Prize for Literature. He died December 20, 1968, in New York City and at his request his ashes were buried in the Garden of Memories Cemetery in Salinas.

Plot Summary

Chapter 1

The Pearl begins as Kino, a Mexican pearl diver in the village of La Paz on the gulf of California, awakes before morning. His wife Juana and child Coyotito lie nearby in their brush house. Kino contentedly listens to the waves on the beach and declares "it was very good." His ancestors had passed their songs down from generation to generation to Kino, who this morning has the "Song of Family" in his mind. Juana rises and makes breakfast for the family, as she does every morning, and sings part of the Family Song.

Suddenly Kino sees a scorpion crawling down one of the ropes that holds the baby's cradle, and a new song, a "Song of Evil," enters his head. He lunges at it but is too late and the scorpion stings Coyotito. Juana immediately tries to suck out the poison from the wound, but the area begins to swell. She and Kino take the baby to the doctor in town, along with many neighbors who have come to watch, but because they have no money, he will not see them. Filled with shame and rage, Kino smashes his fist against the doctor's gate.

Chapter 2

After Kino and his family return to their

fishing village, Juana places a seaweed poultice on the baby's wound and prays that Kino will find a pearl that would pay for the doctor. That afternoon when Kino goes diving, he finds the largest pearl he has ever seen, "The Pearl of the World," "as large as a sea-gull's egg" and as "perfect as the moon," and he howls with joy.

Chapter 3

Soon the entire town knows of the pearl, speculating on what it is worth. All suddenly are interested in Kino as the pearl "stirred up something infinitely black and evil in the town." Kino had become "curiously every man's enemy," but he and Juana are oblivious to the town's dark thoughts. They dream of what they can do with the money they will gain when they sell the pearl, deciding that they will be able to get married and buy new clothes and get their son an education, which will grant him freedom.

Kino, however, begins to hear the "Evil Song" as he thinks others will try to steal the pearl from him and so he makes "a hard skin for himself against the world." When the doctor hears the news, he reminisces of his past life in Paris and decides that he will take Coyotito as a patient and so get his hands on some of the money from the pearl. He comes to the brush house and warns Kino and Juana that the poison may still be inside their son but that he can help. After the doctor forces Coyotito to swallow what he insists is medicine to drive the poison out, Coyotito becomes ill. Soon, however, he appears to recover and the doctor demands payment. Kino determines to sell the pearl the next day. That night, though, someone comes to the hut to try to steal the it. Kino scares him away but not before he is hit in the head. Juana warns that the pearl is a "sin" and will destroy them, but Kino insists it is their only chance to send Coyotito to school.

Chapter 4

The townspeople follow Kino into town on his journey to meet with the pearl buyers and speculate about what they would buy with the money he will earn for it. The first buyer offers only 1000 pesos, claiming that the pearl is "fool's gold" and has little value. When Kino refuses the offer and insists that it is worth 50,000 pesos, the buyer calls others in to make bids, but they also determine the pearl to be worthless. Kino declares that he is being cheated and vows to journey to the capital to sell it even though he is afraid to go there. His neighbors are unsure about whether Kino has been cheated or whether he is being greedy. That evening when Kino is again attacked by robbers outside his brush house, Juana pleads with him to destroy the pearl, but he refuses, insisting that he "is a man" and so can handle any trouble they may face.

Chapter 5

In the middle of the night Juana arises and

takes the pearl to the water, ready to throw it in. Kino, however, stops her just in time, grabs the pearl and beats her in an animalistic rage. On his way back to the brush house, he is sickened by what he has done. On the trail assassins attack him, but this time he kills one of the men. Juana realizes that at this point, "the old life was gone forever." Realizing that he will be accused of murder, Kino decides that they must flee and turns to his brother Juan Tomas and his wife for help. Kino admits, "This pearl has become my soul.... If I give it up I shall lose my soul."

Media Adaptations

- *La Perla*, a Mexican and American production of *The Pearl* was released in 1947. Steinbeck worked on the screenplay and the film was directed by Emilio Fernandez.

- In 2001, Hollywood released

another version of *The Pearl*, starring Richard Harris and Lukas Haas. This film was directed by Alfredo Zacharias.

- An audio version of *The Pearl*, produced by Penguin and read by Hector Elizondo, is available through Audio Books.

Chapter 6

Kino and his family travel up the coast but soon realize that trackers are following them. In an effort to lose them, they head into the mountains. At one point, Kino considers turning himself in to save his family, but Juana convinces him that the trackers would kill all of them to get the pearl. The family stops near caves to rest, but the trackers eventually catch up with them. Under the cover of darkness, Kino tries to jump one of the men while the other two are sleeping. He is able to kill all three, but a random rifle shot during the struggle hits Coyotito, killing him.

Kino and Juana return to La Paz, devastated at the loss of their son, appearing as if "removed from human experience." Hearing the Song of the Family ringing in his ears like "a battle cry," Kino grasps the pearl, which has become "gray and ulcerous" with "evil faces" peering from it. When he tries to give it to Juana, she insists, "no you." Kino then throws it with all of his might into the green water, and it disappears.

Characters

Coyotito

Coyotito, Kino and Juana's infant son, is the catalyst for his parents' obsession with the pearl. Both of his parents want the pearl to help pay for his recovery from the scorpion sting and for his education, so that he will not be limited by the same oppression under which his parents have suffered.

Doctor

The doctor is part of the system that oppresses Kino and his family. The villagers know "his cruelty, his avarice, his appetites," his laziness, and his incompetence. His sense of superiority prompts him to regard Kino and his neighbors as animals and so determines that he need not treat them. Only after he learns of Kino's pearl does he offer help so that he may be able to get his hands on it and regain the luxurious life he has enjoyed in Paris. To that end, he deceives Kino and Juana about Coyotito's illness and his own powers as a healer.

Juan Tomás

Kino's brother Juan Tomás provides Kino with shelter and wise counsel.

Juana

Juana is a dutiful wife who rises every morning to make breakfast for her family. She exhibits a fierce, instinctual need to protect her child as evidenced by her clearheaded response to the scorpion's sting and her insistence that they take him to the doctor, knowing that there is little chance that the doctor will see him yet ready to face the resulting shame. Coyotito is Juana's first baby and so he is "nearly everything there was in [her] world."

Her strength and endurance, however, are her most dominant qualities. Kino "wondered often at the iron in his patient, fragile wife" who "could arch her back in child pain with hardly a cry" and "stand fatigue and hunger almost better than Kino himself." He notes that "in the canoe she was like a strong man." Although patient with and obedient to her husband, she tries to convince him to throw away the pearl when she recognizes the danger it brings.

Her endurance is displayed after Kino beats her. As he stands over her with his teeth bared, she stares as him "with wide unfrightened eyes." She accepts that he had been driven over the edge of reason and decided "she would not resist or even protest." As a result, Kino's rage disappears and is replaced by disgust for what he has done to her.

Juana shows a great and patient understanding of her husband. After he beats her, she feels no anger toward him, recognizing that as a man "he was half insane and half god." She knows that he will "drive his strength against a mountain and plunge his strength against the sea" and that he would inevitably be destroyed by both. Although puzzled by the differences she recognizes between men and women, she "knew them and accepted them and needed them" because as an Indian woman "she could not live without a man." She then determines to follow him, hoping that her reason, caution, and "sense of preservation could cut through Kino's manness and save them all." Juana endures the pain of her injuries as she escapes with Kino and Coyotito.

Her ability to defy her husband by attempting to throw the pearl in the sea while admitting that she could not survive without him reveals her great courage. She is driven by her need to "rescue something of the old peace, of the time before the pearl." Yet after Kino kills his attacker, she shows her resilience when she immediately admits that the past was gone, "and there was no retrieving it. And knowing this, she abandoned the past instantly. There was nothing to do but to save themselves." The death of her child appears to break her, however. As she walks back to the village at the end of the story, "her wide eyes stared inward on herself" and she "was as remote and as removed as Heaven.

Kino

Even though he lives in poverty, Kino is

content at the beginning of the story because he is surrounded by the family he loves. It is only after his child's life is threatened by the scorpion bite that Kino determines that he will rebel against the system that oppresses him.

He is connected to his ancestors through their songs, which he often hears in his head. The frequency of the Family Song and the Enemy Song suggests his strong link to those ancestors as well as to his environment. Kino experiences a combination of rage and fear as he confronts his oppressors, showing strength as well as an intuitive assessment of the reality of his position. He is a proud man who feels shame when he stirs up the courage to challenge that position and is rebuffed.

Like Juana, he is a responsible parent who strives to provide the best life possible for his child. This commitment gives him the courage to rebel against the status quo by calling on the doctor, by refusing to accept the offer from the pearl buyers, and by fleeing the village after he murders one of his attackers. His loyalty is also expressed toward his neighbors when it does not even occur to him to take one of their boats during his escape.

His obsession with the pearl is prompted by his desire for respect and power, but most importantly for the education of his child. He wants to be able to marry Juana, to buy a rifle that can "[break] down the barriers," to dress his family in nice clothes, and finally to enable his son to free himself and his people from subjugation.

Kino's fierce desire to provide for and protect his family reduces him to a primal state. Ironically that desire to provide for them causes him to viciously attack Juana. Later, after he kills his attacker, the narrator concludes that Kino is "an animal now, for hiding, for attacking, and he lived only to preserve himself and his family." This primal nature enables him to escape his trackers, at least initially. The narrator notes that "some ancient thing stirred in Kino.... some animal thing was moving in him so that he was cautious and wary and dangerous." At the end of the story, he appears broken as he retains his primal state. He, along with Juana, appears "removed from human experience." He "carried fear with him" and "he was as dangerous as a rising storm."

Greed

The story has been applauded as a parable that warns of the effects of greed. A parable is a story that is chiefly intended to convey a moral or truth. After Kino finds the pearl, he learns how far others will go, including committing murder, to gain wealth and the power that it brings. All those who hear about the pearl, even his neighbors "suddenly became related to [it], and [it] went into the dreams, the speculations, the schemes, the plans, the futures, the wishes, the needs, the lusts, the hungers, of everyone." And since Kino stood in their way, "he became curiously every man's enemy." Kino recognizes this desire in himself, not for wealth, but for the power the pearl can grant him. He says the pearl is his soul.

Topics for Further Study

- Read Steinbeck's short story "The Chrysanthemums" and compare the main character in it to Juana. Both are strong women but they deal with their husbands in different ways. What do these differences say about their character and their culture? What similarities do you find in both women?

- Stephen Crane's "The Open Boat" is a naturalistic story that focuses on the environmental forces that control human destiny. Compare and contrast these forces with those forces that control Kino and his family.

- Research the history of the Mexican Indians who lived in the La Paz region. How did they become marginalized in Mexican society? What are their lives like today?

- Consider an alternate ending for the story. What would have happened to the family if Coyotito had lived? Do you see any possibility that Kino could achieve his dreams given the constraints of his world? Explain.

Environmental and Biological Determinism

Steinbeck incorporates naturalistic elements in the story through his focus on environmental and biological determinism. Determinism is a way of understanding what causes humans to experience what they do. The assumption is that there are forces (such as race, economic class, environment, and chance) at work that determine the outcome of human events, regardless of human intention and effort to shape events otherwise. Kino's fate is sealed by these forces, which prevent him from escaping the limitations of his world. The most obvious determinants are his social and economic status.

Kino knows that "other forces were set up to destroy" his plan to provide his family with an opportunity to escape oppression. He believes though that these forces are created by the gods, who "do not love men's plans," who "do not love success unless it comes by accident," and who "take their revenge on a man if he be successful through his own efforts." This deterministic view maintains that the individual is powerless to shape his circumstances or to rise above them. Perhaps it is the gods or fate but some arbitrary force beyond the self controls everything.

Since Kino is an Indian and has no education, he does not know how to fight against the ruling class who exploit him in an effort to keep him in his place. He cannot read the medicine packet that the doctor uses to "treat" Coyotito, he does not have the knowledge to judge the real value of the pearl, and he does not know how to find someone who will give him a fair price. He is poor because he is a member of an oppressed race, and so he must live in dangerous conditions where scorpions can pose a risk.

Another dangerous and immediate environmental factor is posed by the greedy men who want to steal his pearl. Kino is almost killed by these attackers until he kills one in self defense. Their greed illustrates the biological forces with which Kino must also grapple.

At least initially, both Kino and Juana are committed to their dreams. Juana becomes "a lioness" when her baby is stung by the scorpion, which ironically triggers the path to his destruction. Her fierce sense of protection prompts her to convince Kino to go to the doctor and later to find the biggest pearl he can catch so that they will have the money to cure their child.

After Kino finds the pearl, his own biology takes over as he becomes filled with a hatred that "raged and flamed in back of his eyes, and fear too, for the hundreds of years of subjugation were cut deep in him." That rage, coupled with his own instinct to provide the best for his family, urges him on even as murderers wait outside his brush house to attack him. These urges become obsessions as his brain "burns" in dreams of his son's future. Even after Juana warns him of the dangers of keeping the pearl, Kino insists he will not give it up, claiming "this is our one chance.... Our son must go to school. He must break out of the pot that holds us in."

His obsession with the pearl prompts him to violently attack Juana when she tries to throw it back into the sea. His brain, "red hot with anger," reverts to a primal state as he punches and kicks her with "his teeth bared" and hissing "like a snake." These dual forces, Kino's environment and his own biology conspire against him: his burning desire for a better life for his family and the oppression of the ruling class that forces him into subjugation ultimately shape his destiny.

Parable

A parable is a story designed to illustrate a lesson or moral. Steinbeck notes at the beginning of *The Pearl* that the story of Kino and the pearl has been told so often, "it has taken root in every man's mind" and "heart." He characterizes the story as a parable when he explains that "there are only good and bad things and black and white things and good and evil things and no in-between anywhere."

On one level, the story can be viewed as an allegory of good and evil, with Kino and his family representing good, and those who try to steal the pearl from him as evil. In this reading, the lesson or moral focuses on how the pearl inspires greed. However, there are some "in-between things" that suggest a more complex reflection of reality, especially in Steinbeck's exploration of the interplay of oppression and rebellion.

Symbolism

The dominant symbol in the novel is the pearl. Initially it is "the Pearl of the World," "as large as a sea gull's egg" and as "perfect as the moon"; it represents a bright future for Kino and his family. Kino sees the pearl as providing the "music of promise and delight" with its "guarantee of the future, of comfort, of security." It promised "a poultice against illness and a wall against insult. It closed a door on hunger." As it inspires greed in the hearts of others, however, and Kino is forced to face the consequences of that greed, the pearl transforms into a "gray and ulcerous" object with "evil faces" peering from it."

The scorpion becomes a symbol of this transformation. Like the scorpion's sting, the pearl infects those who come into contact with it because it stimulates their greed. They turn into predators symbolized by the story's nighttime setting, when "mice crept about on the ground and the little night hawks hunted them silently." The darkness is filled with a "poisonous air." At the beginning of the story, the attacks that Kino must fend off are symbolized by the two roosters near his house, who "bowed and feinted at each other with squared wings and neck feathers ruffed out."

Pearl Diving in La Paz

La Paz (meaning "peace" in Spanish) is in the Mexican state of Southern Baja California on the Sea of Cortez. For several centuries, the area was famous for its pearl diving and was known as "The City of Pearls." The oyster beds, however, became diseased and died out in the middle of the twentieth century.

In the mid 1900s, approximately 800 divers would submerge themselves in the waters off La Paz at depths of up to 12 fathoms. Divers had to tear the oysters by hand from their beds, a process that often left their hands with deep cuts and gashes. The number of divers decreased to about 200 by the end of the century as the oyster population declined and divers lost their lives due to accidents and shark attacks.

Compare & Contrast

- **1940s:** World War II results from the rise of totalitarian regimes in Germany, Italy, and Japan. More than two hundred countries band together to fight against the militaristic expansion of these totalitarian regimes.

Today: The United States, with the help of coalition forces, invades Iraq in 2003, acting upon information that Iraq supposedly poses a threat and has weapons of mass destruction. During 2004, several coalition allies pull out of Iraq, and the supposed weapons of mass destruction are not found. More than one thousand U.S. military persons are killed in the ongoing U.S. occupation; tens of thousands of Iraqis are killed.

- **1940s:** Poor Mexicans who cannot make enough money to survive in their homeland emigrate to the United States in search of better jobs.
  Today: Mexicans continue to cross the border. U.S. officials try to guard national borders, especially after terrorist attacks on September 11, 2001, but the federal government also discusses ways to allow Mexicans in the United States to find temporary employment.

- **1940s:** Steinbeck uses naturalism and the form of the parable in *The Pearl*. Important literary styles are realism, naturalism, modernism.
  Today: Two popular literary forms are psychological realism and

autobiography, which may be confessional, humorous, or historical. Historical mysteries are popular as proven by the bestseller, *The Da Vinci Code*.

Naturalism

Naturalism is a literary movement that emerged in the late nineteenth and early twentieth centuries in France, England, and the United States. Writers included in this group, such as Emile Zola, Thomas Hardy, and the Americans Stephen Crane and Theodore Dreiser, write about biological and/or environmental determinism that prevents their characters from achieving the goals they seek. These characters' plans for the future and their choices (the exercise of their free will) are all swamped by forces beyond their control. For example, in *The Red Badge of Courage* Crane depicts how one Civil War soldier is overwhelmed by the U.S. political and military conflict. Zola's and Dreiser's work include this type of environmental determinism coupled with an exploration of the influences of heredity in their portraits of ordinary men and women engaged in a relentless and brutal struggle for survival.

World War II

The world witnessed a decade of aggression in

the 1930s that culminated in the 1939 onset of World War II. This war resulted from the rise of totalitarian regimes in Germany, Italy, and Japan. These militaristic regimes gained control, in part, as a result of a global economic depression and from the conditions created by the peace settlements following World War I, called the Treaty of Versailles. The dictatorships established in these three countries were committed to territorial expansion. In Germany Hitler strengthened the army during the late 1930s. In 1936 Benito Mussolini's Italian troops took Ethiopia. From 1936 to 1939 Spain was engaged in civil war involving Francisco Franco's fascist army, aided by Germany and Italy. In March 1938 Germany annexed Austria and in March 1939 occupied Czechoslovakia. Italy took Albania in April 1939. One week after Nazi Germany and the U.S.S.R. signed the Treaty of Nonaggression, on September 1, 1939, Germany invaded Poland. On September 3, 1939, Britain and France declared war on Germany after a U-boat sank the British ship *Athenia* off the coast of Ireland. Another British ship, *Courageous*, was sunk on September 19. All the members of the British Commonwealth, except Ireland, soon joined Britain and France in their declaration of war against Germany.

On December 7, 1941, Japan attacked the U.S. military base in Pearl Harbor, Hawaii. As a result of the four-hour attack, approximately 2,400 Americans died and 1300 were wounded. Three days later, Germany and Italy declared war on the United States. The total number of European casualties by the end of the war was approximately 40,000,000. More than 400,000 Americans died.

Critical Overview

"The Pearl of the World" first appeared in *The Women's Home Companion* in 1945. The 1947 revised version, *The Pearl*, gained immediate critical and popular attention. During the following years, the novella was attacked by some, such as Warren French in his article on Steinbeck, as being too "sentimental." Many readers, however, continued throughout the twentieth century to praise the story's themes and construction.

Ernest E. Karsten Jr., in his 1965 article on *The Pearl*, praises its "combination of simple story, strongly established symbolism, social commentary, and important themes," and argues that Steinbeck's "beautiful writing makes this a literary work that may well become a classic and certainly as fine an introduction to the genre as could be found."

In his 1947 review of the novella for the *New York Times*, Carlos Baker writes that the novella "fits as neatly into the list of Steinbeck's books as the last gem in a carefully matched necklace." Orville Prescott, in his review for the same paper, commends Steinbeck's "artful simplicity exactly suitable to his theme" and insists that it is "the best book which Mr. Steinbeck has written since "The Red Pony" and *The Grapes of Wrath*." Prescott especially praises the characterizations in the book, noting that Kino's "devotion to his family and his courage in the face of death are deeply moving" and that these traits give the novella "a universally human quality, for they are the virtues which men everywhere have always admired above all others."

What Do I Read Next?

- Stephen Crane's short story "The Open Boat" (1898) depicts the desperation of four ship-wrecked seamen who are controlled by the whims of the sea.

- *The Awakening* (1899) is Kate Chopin's feminist novel of a young married woman who confronts the conflicting demands of housewife and artist and inevitably suffers the consequences of trying to establish herself as an independent spirit in a world governed by strict codes of conduct.

- In *The Log from the Sea of Cortez*, Steinbeck relates the folk tale that inspired his writing of *The Pearl*.

- Steinbeck's *The Grapes of Wrath* (1939) focuses on a group of people forced to leave their homes during the Great Depression and travel to California where they struggle to survive as migrant workers.

Sources

Astro, Richard, "John Steinbeck," in *Dictionary of Literary Biography*, Vol. 9, *American Novelists, 1910–1945*, Gale Research, 1981, pp. 43-68.

Baker, Carlos, "Steinbeck at the Top of His Form," in the *New York Times*, November 30, 1947, pp. BR4, 52.

French, Warren, "John Steinbeck," in *Twayne's United States Authors Series Online*, G. K. Hall, 1999.

Karsten, Ernest E., Jr., "Thematic Structure in *The Pearl*," in *English Journal*, Vol. 54, No. 1, January 1965, pp. 1-7.

Prescott, Orville, "Books of the Times," in the *New York Times*, November 24, 1947, p. 21.

Steinbeck, John, *East of Eden*, Penguin, 1992.

—————, *The Pearl*, in *The Short Novels of John Steinbeck*, Viking, 1953, pp. 471-527.

Further Reading

Mitchell, Marilyn H., "Steinbeck's Strong Women: Feminine Identity in the Short Stories," in *John Steinbeck: A Study of the Short Fiction*, edited by R. S. Hughes, Twayne, 1989, pp. 154-66.

> Mitchell looks at strong women in Steinbeck's fiction.

Owens, Lois, *John Steinbeck's Re-Vision of America*, University of Georgia Press, 1985.

> Owens analyzes the changes in Steinbeck's vision of America over the course of his literary career.

Timmerman, John, "Steinbeck's Environmental Ethic: Humanity and Harmony with the Land," in *Steinbeck and the Environment: Interdisciplinary Approaches*, edited by Susan F. Beegel, Susan Shillinglaw, and Wesley N. Tiffney Jr., University of Alabama Press, 1997, pp. 310-22.

> Timmerman examines Steinbeck's vision of the environment and people's relationship to it.

Tuttleton, James W., "Steinbeck Remembered," in the *New Criterion*, Vol. 13, No. 7, March 1995, pp. 22-28.

> Tuttleton presents a comprehensive overview of Steinbeck's career and reputation.